The not So Striped Tiger

Whitley Rae Stokes

There is an amazon eBook that goes

along with this paper back copy.

Thank you for purchasing

and I hope you enjoy!

To Genevieve and Thaddeus,

Dori loves you so much. In a world where everyone wants to be the same, know that it is enough just to be YOU!

I am Tim the Tiger, and I don't have any

stripes.

It's as if someone

took them with one big swipe.

9 look at all my friends
who are colored with

orange

black and

white

but because I look different,

they are sometimes not so nice.

They say words that hurt my feelings and

give me funny stares.

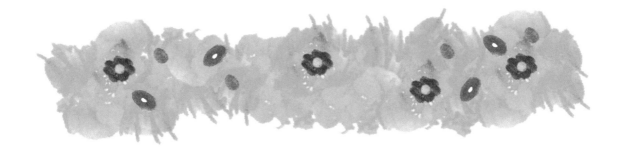

It makes me feel sad and like they

don't even care.

Who would want to hang out with

a tiger as

DIFFERENT

as me?

Sometimes I just wish they would

let me be.

What matters is what's in your heart, not what's on the outside. I keep my head held high to show my pride.

It doesn't matter if I'm...

pink

purple

blue.

It's okay to be unique, it is what makes you,

In a world where

EVERYONE

wants to be the same, be

DIFFERENT.

It's okay!

Facts About Tigers

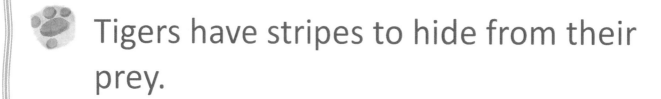 Tigers have stripes to hide from their prey.

Tigers are the largest cat species in the word and third largest carnivore.

Like human fingerprints. No two tigers have the same stripes.

A Tigers tail is about 3 feet long and helps them balance when making tight turns.

Hear Me Roar

The objective of this activity is to encourage students to be inclusive and support each other no matter what differences they have. This is to build up a sense of community within a home, classroom, or school. When the child is caught giving a compliment, including another students, or using kind words the student will receive a reward. You can use tiger stickers, tiger stuffed animal, or any other incentive. Once a student receives the award, it is their job to pass it along to another student that show these same characteristics.

Science Activity

Objective: To study the relationship between predator/prey and analyze the effects of camouflaging on the survival of a species.

Materials:
- Cut out picture of black and white rabbit for you to color
- Markers/crayons/colored pencils
- An adult to act as the "predator"

Procedure:
- The teacher will provide the student with a black and white rabbit for them to color.
- The student will pick a place in the room/house that they want their rabbit to "hide". (needs to be in plain view and not behind and object-the goal is to use camouflage make it blend into its surroundings)
- The student will color the rabbit to match the background where they tape their picture.
- Once the students have camouflaged their rabbit an adult will enter the room and try to find the "prey".

Art Activity

By: Thaddeus

In this activity, you will be making a paper plate tiger.

Materials:
- Paper plate
- construction paper/ tissue paper
- Scissors
- Glue

You can use scissors, or the student can work on tearing the paper which is a pre-cutting skill.

Comprehension questions

1. What is the main character's name?
   a. Tim
   b. Tony
   c. Tom

2. At the beginning of the story Tim was
   _____ about not having stripes.

   a. Happy
   b. Sad
   c. Angry

3. What kind of animal is Tim?
   a. Lion
   b. Tiger
   c. Giraffe

Comprehension questions

4. At the end of the story how does Tim feel about not having stripes?
   a. Happy
   b. Sad
   c. Angry

5. What is Tim missing in the story?
   a. A toy
   b. His stripes
   c. His friend

Vocabulary

<u>Pride:</u> to be proud of.

<u>Unique:</u> being the only one of its kind.

<u>Swipe:</u> to grab quickly.

<u>Stare:</u> prolonged gaze or look.

What is Williams Syndrome?

Williams syndrome is a genetic condition that is present at birth. It is characterized by medical problems, including cardiovascular disease, developmental delays, and learning challenges. These often occur side by side with verbal abilities, highly social personalities, and an affinity for music. Williams Syndrome occurs equally in males and females and in all cultures worldwide.